TIPs for Sips

Thoughts, Inspirations, and Parables
to Start Your Day

Tresa M. Sullivan

Tresa M. Sullivan

TIPs for Sips

Thoughts, Inspirations, and Parables to Start Your Day

Tresa M. Sullivan

Pearly Gates Publishing, LLC, Houston, Texas (USA)

TIPs for Sips

TIPS for Sips:
Thoughts, Inspirations, and Parables to Start Your Day

Copyright © 2021
Tresa M. Sullivan

All Rights Reserved.
No portion of this publication may be reproduced, stored in an electronic system, or transmitted in any form or by any means (electronic, mechanical, photocopy, recording, or otherwise) without written permission from the author or publisher. Brief quotations may be used in literary reviews.

Print ISBN: 978-1-948853-23-1
Digital ISBN: 978-1-948853-24-8
Library of Congress Control Number: 2021903822

Scripture references are used and taken from the King James Version of the Holy Bible via Zondervan at Biblegateway.com. Public Domain.

For information and bulk ordering, contact:
Pearly Gates Publishing, LLC
Angela Edwards, CEO
P.O. Box 62287
Houston, TX 77205
BestSeller@PearlyGatesPublishing.com

What Others Are Saying...

"Tresa is such a wise woman who has a way with words. If only I could borrow that skill, I would be able to clearly articulate and paint an accurate picture of all that embodies Tresa Sullivan. However, I honestly do not believe even the most skilled scholar could formulate the perfect words to describe this woman's beautiful nature. With a heart as pure as they come, Tresa not only lights up the page with her words, but she also brings life to people by continuously pouring words of encouragement, love, and wisdom into all and any who have had the pleasure of knowing her intimately. She is intelligent and gifted with the ability to teach and stimulate the minds of others. Tresa is genuine, with key principles being her honesty and authenticity. They are quite refreshing traits. She is a lot of things and wears a lot of hats. I feel blessed that one of those roles is being my aunt."
~ **Gabrielle K. Parks, CEO**
PamperedByParks

****

"The author—my sister-in-law—is inspiring, powerful, and graceful! She has allowed us a peek into her soul, where her innermost thoughts and feelings reside. Once cannot help but be lured in, wanting to read more, feel more, and understand more. Her faith in God is present in all she does, and her love of life is evident every single day."
~ **Kim Dooley**

****

"Tresa is an insightful woman of God. She is a visionary with a plan of action led by her faith. Her challenges are viewed as opportunities, which shine a bright light in the darkness. She is a delight to have in your presence. On the pages of this book, you will find basic yet profound principles of life. The words will leave you thinking and reflecting on various areas of your own life. Read slowly. Take it all in. It is powerful!"
~ **Karen Albert Warren, PhD**

****

"My sister, Tresa, has always been encouraging to others. She is open and honest with her feelings. I am very proud of her for following her dreams and being an inspiration for others. I was particularly drawn to the entry, "Two Wrongs." Her analogy is spot on: Trying to get even only makes it worse. Furthermore, she is so right about God. I would not want to play that game with Him because He wins every time."
~ **Rhonda Mays**

Dedication

This book is dedicated to my dad,
Robert F. Sheard, Sr.

If my words mean to anyone a tenth of what your words meant to me, I have found my life's calling and my time is very well spent. My aim today and always is to, as you always said,
"Let nothing separate you from the love of God."

Acknowledgments

I would like to thank my husband and sons for their unwavering support and for encouraging me to put my thoughts in writing.

To Randy: Thank you for always inspiring me to elevate. You not only believe in me, but also continuously insist that I do what I love and be proud of it.

To Myles: Thank you for adding to that inspiration and reminding me that the limits I choose to live within are not God's limitations for me. You ALWAYS hold me accountable, and for that, I am very appreciative.

To Cameron: Thank you for affording me the opportunity to put my faith in action and live in God's Word. You challenge my thoughts and bring new waves of perspective to my life. Thank you for the two entries that will forever belong to Ka$h.

I would also like to thank my mom, Mattie Sheard, and my sisters, Deborah West, Rena Dicus, and Felecia Sheard-Parks for listening to or reading my thoughts each day. You convinced me my words were worth sharing and that others would appreciate them. Without you, this would not have been a project and certainly never would have come into fruition. I cannot fail to say thank you to the rest of the family, Robert Jr., Marvin, Alvin, John, Earl, and Rhonda for being an integral part of my life.

Tresa M. Sullivan

Preface

For as long as I can remember, I have held God's canvas in high regard. I cherish the gift of vision—not just the ability to observe with my eyes but also the ability to discern and observe with my heart. I take mental pictures and often actual photos because I know otherwise, I will never see things exactly the same twice. I feel the same way about God's Word and hold it close to my heart.

I recently decided to share with you my interpretations of His words and His canvas within these pages.

Enjoy, and may you be blessed beyond measure!

Introduction

On the pages of *TIPs for Sips*, you will encounter some of the author's daily thoughts and musings. As she sits with her morning coffee, afternoon tea, or evening hot chocolate, she receives random, Spirit-inspired teachings when alone and in her quiet time. From the rising of the sun, to the going down of the same, Tresa's mind is filled with reflections that often lead her to the Throne of Grace.

Tresa desires to give you something to ponder each day. As you read, perhaps one of her TIPs will provide confirmation or a fresh perspective about something you have had on your mind.

Tresa states, "If only one person finds this piece of literary art helpful, I am most grateful to God for affording me the opportunity to share the TIPs He has entrusted to me." She shares freely and welcomes agreement or disagreement and thoughtful conversations. Enjoy each "Sipping Session"!

Tresa M. Sullivan

Table of Contents

What Others Are Saying… vi

Dedication viii

Acknowledgments ix

Preface x

Introduction xi

Not Being Captive Did Not Make Me Free xviii

Sipping Session One 1
   Taking Care of Me First

Sipping Session Two 5
   Shall We Question Our Faith— or Our Prayers?

Sipping Session Three 9
   That Quiet Place

Sipping Session Four 12
   Ingest, Digest, Expel, and Repeat

Sipping Session Five 15
   Admittance Comes Before the Blame Game

Sipping Session Six 18
   Fly from the Nest, Don't Fall

Sipping Session Seven 21
   Two Wrongs

Sipping Session Eight 24
   Background and Light

Sipping Session Nine 28
   Forgiving

TIPs for Sips

Sipping Session Ten 32
   Are You Chasing or Running?

Sipping Session Eleven 35
   The Power of Repetition

Sipping Session Twelve 38
   Things I Have Learned

Sipping Session Thirteen 43
   Change the Light, Not the Lampshade

Sipping Session Fourteen 46
   If But One

Sipping Session Fifteen 49
   Trees and Lichens?

Sipping Session Sixteen 53
   Sometimes, You Don't Get a Second Chance

Sipping Session Seventeen 56
   In the Woods

Sipping Session Eighteen 60
   To Dine with Danger

Sipping Session Nineteen 64
   I Don't Know His Name

Sipping Session Twenty 67
   Rise and Shine

Sipping Session Twenty-One 70
   Sort Your Friends

Sipping Session Twenty-Two 74
   Courage

Sipping Session Twenty-Three..77
  Problems

Sipping Session Twenty-Four...80
  With You

Sipping Session Twenty-Five 83
  Riches

Sipping Session Twenty-Six 86
  Footstool

Sipping Session Twenty-Seven 89
  For a Limited Time Only

Sipping Session Twenty-Eight...92
  Ticket for Nothing and the Ride Is Free

Sipping Session Twenty-Nine 95
  What Are You Wearing Today?

Sipping Session Thirty 98
  I Choose to Live in the Woods

Sipping Session Thirty-One..101
  Voices and Words

Sipping Session Thirty-Two 107
  Water My Soul

Sipping Session Thirty-Three 110
  Value Added

Sipping Session Thirty-Four...113
  Faith Conquers Fear

Sipping Session Thirty-Five..116
  What Are You Chasing?

TIPs for Sips

Sipping Session Thirty-Six 119
    The Name "Jesus"

Sipping Session Thirty-Seven 122
    Be Kind

Sipping Session Thirty-Eight 125
    'No' is Not a Bad Word

Sipping Session Thirty-Nine 128
    Let Wisdom Be Your Defense

Sipping Session Forty 131
    Doesn't Cost You Anything

Sipping Session Forty-One 134
    Don't Let Denomination Become Abomination

Sipping Session Forty-Two 137
    Tame or Flame

Sipping Session Forty-Three 140
    Love Deeply

Sipping Session Forty-Four 143
    The Light Within

Sipping Session Forty-Five 146
    Games

Sipping Session Forty-Six 149
    Take Time to Pay Attention

Sipping Session Forty-Seven 152
    What's on Your Thirds?

Sipping Session Forty-Eight 155
    Your Survival Kit

Sipping Session Forty-Nine 158
    You Are the Lifeline

Sipping Session Fifty 161
    Treat Your Soul Like You Treat Your Hair, Not Your Nails

Sipping Session Fifty-One 165
    The Unintentional Gardener

Sipping Session Fifty-Two 169
    What You See is What You Get

Sipping Session Fifty-Three 172
    Worry About Yourself

Sipping Session Fifty-Four 176
    Speaking of Rain…

Sipping Session Fifty-Five 179
    How Deep Is Your Love?

Sipping Session Fifty-Six 182
    Five Senses

Sipping Session Fifty-Seven 186
    The Clearing

Sipping Session Fifty-Eight 189
    If the Shoe Fits…

Sipping Session Fifty-Nine 192
    It's Not a Matter of Freedom, It's a Matter of Free Dum (Dum)

Sipping Session Sixty 196
    My Account

Sipping Session Sixty-One 199
    Measured Steps, One Day at a Time

TIPs for Sips

Sipping Session Sixty-Two 202
    Before You Check Your Carry-On, Check Your Baggage

Sipping Session Sixty-Three 205
    Which Will You Be?

Bonus 208
    Remember When?

About the Author 211

Appendix 212

Tresa M. Sullivan

Not Being Captive Did Not Make Me Free

A Poem By KA$H and Tresa

Never twain shall the two of us be, for I am you, and you are me. You slay the day; I fight the night; how could I not know we fight the same fight. Eyes wide open, but I could not see, not being captive did not make me free.

I run with the same crew; one too crude for you, but they pledged me loyalty. I don't know how this happened, we seemed always at odds and could not get it right. Never twain shall the two of us be, for I am you, and you are me.

There were many a day you went your own way, in spite of my unspoken plea. You always returned with hope in your eyes, encouraging me to take flight. Eyes wide open, but I could not see, not being captive did not make me free.

To succeed I must sever all that hinders progress and let what is be. I know you support me and that makes it all alright. Never twain shall the two of us be, for I am you, and you are me.

You said, "Don't let up, do what you do. Let everyone see, you know what you are doing, you are not fly by night, your vision is right." Eyes wide open, but I could not see, not being captive did not make me free.

I look around, you are here by my side, but where else would you be? Nothing is holding me back; I am truly free. I'm happy, content, in utter delight! Never twain shall the two of us be, for I am you, and you are me. Eyes wide open, but I could not see, not being captive did not make me free!

Sipping Session One

Taking Care of Me First

I strongly believe I have to make sure I can take care of myself in order to be of assistance to anyone else. I do not have a problem saying no when it is not in my best interest. In fact, saying no sometimes feels really good.

Bear with me; this is not as selfish as it may seem, so hear me out…

Before takeoff on an airplane or push-off on a ship, passengers are given safety instructions. Although representatives from the different modes of transportation may use different words, the message conveyed is the same: Make sure you are safe before helping others. That is because you cannot help anyone else if you are incapacitated. The same applies to mental, physical, and spiritual health, and the sustenance you provide others. For example, to feed someone spiritually, your spirit must first be well-nourished.

Do you sometimes feel like you are missing something but cannot pinpoint what it is? That's because being well-nourished spiritually equates to having a balanced mind, body, and soul. You must feed each area of your life with the proper nutrients in order to help others. Now, don't worry: God is not expecting you to do it all alone. He is always there, and He sends others to assist.

We are all unique individuals who require different nutrients. The interesting thing about the process is that we can nourish ourselves simultaneously while nourishing others (and being nourished by others). However, when we are not up to par, we cannot get someone else there.

So, take good care of yourself, whether that be:

- Quiet time and moments with God.
- Speaking to God.
- Just listening to God.
- Studying God's Word.
- Reading a book for entertainment.
- Exercise.
- Listening to music and/or dancing.
- Singing your favorite song.
- Working in the yard/garden.
- Community service.
- Eating a nutritious meal.
- Having a special treat.
- Taking a stroll.
- Watching a little bit of television.
- Conversing with family and friends.
- Taking a nice, hot bath/shower.
- Getting your hair and nails done.
- Buying something nice for yourself or someone else.
- Saying "no" to a request.
- Just doing nothing at all.

Surely, by now, you have gotten my point. Taking care of yourself first will make it amazingly easier to take care of someone else.

NOTE: It may not always be easy, but it will be easier.

Tresa M. Sullivan

Time for Reflection: Encourage Yourself

Sipping Session Two

Shall We Question Our Faith— or Our Prayers?

Are your prayers based on your faith, or are they based on what you desire? Are your prayers causing you to question your faith? If so, it is time to reset. If your prayers are not being answered, then your faith should cause you to question your prayers.

We often ask God for things and honestly hope for and expect them. Yet sometimes we feel like our faith is lacking because we do not receive that for which we ask. Have you ever said, "Lord, I am doing my best. Why is this happening to me? Give me more faith, please!"? Have you ever found yourself desperate or feeling hopeless, even after your best efforts? You may even say to yourself, "I must not have enough faith. I really believe in my heart God can do it, but it is not happening." If you have ever spoken those or similar words, perhaps it is not your faith that you should question. Instead, question your prayers.

"Ye ask, and receive not, because ye ask amiss, that ye may consume it upon your lusts" (James 4:3).

That passage comes to mind when I start feeling that way, especially when I know I am not asking out of sensual lust but a desire of my heart. Over time, I realized that what I ask God for may not be His desire for me. Thus, I have learned to focus my prayers first on being grateful and thanking God for what I have, then asking Him to continue to provide my needs. I never cease to thank God for His grace and mercy and always pray that He keeps my soul in the shadow of His wing. There can be nothing amiss in that request.

In exchange for His blessings, I will gladly take what comes my way, for I know the truth — no matter how tough it may seem:

God will never allow more than I can bear. Even then, He is always there for me. So, when it seems like your prayers are not being answered, do not lose your faith; question your prayers.

Let Thy will be done, my Lord.

Time for Reflection: Encourage Yourself

Sipping Session Three

That Quiet Place

Have you ever been in a crowded restaurant, classroom, auditorium, or any other place with a large group of people and noticed that every conversation around you seems like a foreign language or just babbling? You must literally and intentionally tune out what is going on around you just so you can focus on your own conversation. That is the way life is today. The world is, indeed, a noisy and busy place.

To have a good one-on-one conversation with God, you must find a quiet place and block out everything else. You need a quiet place so you can focus on what you need to discuss with Him and to hear what He directs you to do. Intentionally free your mind of all the clutter. Close your eyes and talk to Him.

Remember: It is a one-on-one conversation, not a one-way conversation.

Once you thank Him for His grace and mercy, pause for a moment. Feel the calmness and peace that starts from the crown of your head and moves through your whole body. Then, thank Him again and, instead of asking for things, ask Him what He desires of you. Continue to seek a clean heart and pure mind in that place of serenity. You will begin to notice small changes in your daily life that will eventually amount to major changes.

Retreat to your quiet place regularly. During a crisis, approach God's throne early. You do not have to try to converse for long periods of time, just honest periods of time. You will discover that you handle challenging situations a lot better than you ever thought you could.

TIPs for Sips

Time for Reflection: Encourage Yourself

Sipping Session Four

Ingest, Digest, Expel, and Repeat

TIPs for Sips

The process of life — not to be confused with the stages of life — is an integral part of human development. Your spiritual being follows the same process flow as your natural body. However, instead of food and water, your spirit/soul ingests God's Word and guidance. Just as you ingest, digest, and expel food, your spirit ingests the Word through reading, hearing, listening (yes, there is a difference), and observation. It then processes the Word, just as your body digests food.

The expulsion of the Word is actualized through your behaviors and what you say. Just as your natural body becomes better at certain activities with repetition, so does your spirit with the repeating of good works. So, as you exercise your natural body for health reasons, exercise your spirit/soul for spiritual warfare.

When your body does not expel digested food, you become weak and ill. Your spirit is much the same. When you ingest God's Word and keep it to yourself, your spirit becomes weak and feeble, which opens the door to reverting to old, ungodly ways. Do not mistreat your body and soul. Read the Word, study it, reread it, and exercise it. Apply it to all you do. You will find the more you consciously refer to the Word and apply it, it becomes second-nature, and you do it without thinking. Ingest, digest, expel, and repeat.

Time for Reflection: Encourage Yourself

Sipping Session Five

Admittance Comes Before the Blame Game

In life, some have a tendency to blame other people for their problems and issues. They sulk and sometimes stay in a rut for years because, whether real or imagined, they think their circumstances are dictated by others' actions. They use someone else's actions as an excuse for not addressing the fact that they have a problem. In order for them to move forward, they must admit something is wrong. It is quite possible for someone else to be the blame for being put in a particular predicament; however, one takes ownership of the predicament when no action is taken to change the conditions or circumstances. Often, there is something that needs to be taken care of before the "Blame Game" starts: Denial.

Sometimes, people are in complete denial that a problem exists. You can bet, if someone you know is in a state of denial, more than likely, they lay the blame for their issues at someone else's feet.

Before you start playing the "Blame Game," take some time today to conduct a self-examination. Take a hard look within. Do you have a problem or issue? Are you contributing to a problem or enabling someone? Admitting a problem is the first step to resolving it.

Do not blame anyone for your problems—AND before you start listing other people's problems, remember to do a self-exam to "first cast out the beam out of thine own eye; and then shalt thou see clearly to cast out the mote out of thy brother's eye" (Matthew 7:5).

TIPs for Sips

Time for Reflection: Encourage Yourself

Sipping Session Six

Fly from the Nest, Don't Fall

TIPs for Sips

Little bird, you have lived in the nest for some time. You were nourished daily. Your bones are strong. The hollowness is filled with the blood of Jesus, which adds no burden to your flight. Your wings are nicely feathered. Only you can determine your lift.

The thermal lift involves raising your hands and arms high into the shape of the letter 'V,' which gives praise and receives victory. That is where your effort comes into play. You are working to move to the next stage of your lift, the gentle glide. Straight arms give thanks and bring mercy and grace. You are now soaring on God's grace and delighting in the peace of the Lord. You complete your heavy lift and are gracefully taking a break.

The aforementioned are the two stages of spiritual lift in which you want to stay. The downward 'V' is the 'N' in "No." It is your descent. It is your faltering, being carried away by the cares of the world. Never fear because you still have trust. While you are faltering, use trust (faith and prayer) to fight the cares and drag of the world. What is drag? It is what happens when you encounter friction (trials and tribulations), and those things are trying to bring you to the ground. It is your trust that pushes you forward.

You are strong. Your aerodynamic build (constructed of belief, faith, prayer, good works, and love) will help you have a smooth touchdown when you falter, and an even smoother takeoff so that you can build a nest and begin feeding others.

Remember: You control your lift, so fly from the nest, don't fall.

Tresa M. Sullivan

Time for Reflection: Encourage Yourself

Sipping Session Seven

Two Wrongs

Tit-for-tat. An eye for an eye. What's good for the goose is good for the gander. A tooth for a tooth. They are all age-old sayings. People often use them to make themselves feel better about a premeditated act or behavior that is often as injurious to themselves as it is to the intended target.

If we really examine and study that ideology, we will clearly see that kind of thinking results in, "What's bad for the goose is bad for the gander." Obviously, a tooth for a tooth does not replace the tooth; it only means two teeth are now missing. Tit-for-tat lends itself to two jerks. Most importantly, an eye for an eye makes for the blind leading the blind, which means no one can see clearly.

So, let's be clear: Two wrongs do not make a right; it only makes two wrongs. One wrong is no less wrong than the other, and both may lead to the wrong destination.

Just think: If God decided to play "Even-Stevens," we would all be lost.

TIPs for Sips

Time for Reflection: Encourage Yourself

Sipping Session Eight

Background and Light

TIPs for Sips

While getting dressed one day, I happened to look in the mirror at what appeared to be something odd on my face, so I leaned in closer to examine. When I did, I noticed I had a gray hair in my mustache. I flipped on the light and got even closer to the mirror. I then noticed I had not only one, but about four gray hairs. I've had a light shade of mustache just about all of my life, so I was not surprised by that. The gray hairs, however, were a problem.

I recall how, in the past, I would mention having a mustache to people. Their response was always, "You don't have a mustache." That was because they could not see it by just glancing at me. (How often do people examine others that closely?) It is fine that people do not notice my mustache, and it really does not bother me that I have one. Even as a woman, although I know it is there, I do not particularly care about its presence.

Although it has not bothered me in the past, now that the hairs are turning gray, it is a little bothersome because it looks like there is something on my face. It has not changed me as a person, but my skin gives the mustache a background color that highlights the gray hairs. When a little light is added to the background color of my skin, it makes the mustache plain for all to see.

While staring in the mirror that day, I thought about how much people are like my mustache. If you really want to find out about someone, add a little background color. Do not presume to know or understand someone based on what you see on the surface. Do a little background work, and you may find what you know or see is not the person's essence. What you see could be hiding some really great or really bad characteristics. The background color will provide a great deal of information. Putting a little light (situational awareness) on them will reveal some reasoning behind some of the things you found when adding the background. It may not make the person perfect or warrant complete dismissal of them, and you may not agree with what you learn, but perhaps you can gain a better understanding. However, should you find anything that should not be, it is up to you to make a conscious decision as to where you will stand.

Background and good lighting bring clarity to whatever is in your field of vision — good or bad. Be mindful and, while you are applying the light to someone else, include yourself.

TIPs for Sips

Time for Reflection: Encourage Yourself

Sipping Session Nine

Forgiving

Today's thought is often a tough subject for many, so let's get right to it.

Forgiving. It is tough because it is hard to do, and sometimes, people do not know how. People may utter the words but fail to actually follow through in both actions and heart.

When you forgive someone, you relinquish what is sometimes a right. You voluntarily take action to release what may be hate, confusion, anger, or resentment—emotions you may own for a good reason. You not only do it for the perpetrator but also for yourself. For some, the problem with forgiveness may be twofold:

1. Many people say they forgive someone but harbor unhealthy feelings, which may be done subconsciously.
2. Some people may forgive the perpetrator but create feelings of guilt for themselves. That, too, may be done subconsciously.

We relinquish the desire for requital but hold on to the feelings of resentment, and because we don't forget, when the memories return, they often trigger uneasiness within ourselves. When that happens, we cannot figure out why we cannot move on in life.

Please don't misinterpret what I am saying here. I am not saying to forget about hurtful things. I am, however, saying use the experience to grow.

Injury, injustice, mental harm, mistakes, and other offenses are often valid reasons for anger and resentment, but what does that anger solve? In many instances, those feelings build brick walls between our perpetrator and us. They sometimes even build walls between us and innocent people, and the world in general. To survive and thrive, we must not focus on forgetting but actually forgiving others, thereby relieving ourselves of undeserved and misplaced guilt.

While no one deserves injustice or harm from injustice, we must use what we don't forget as a tool for living. From pain and harm sometimes comes wisdom. One thing is for certain: If we don't forgive, we will not be forgiven.

Time for Reflection: Encourage Yourself

Tresa M. Sullivan

Sipping Session Ten

Are You Chasing or Running?

Have you ever found yourself sitting in a chair (at home or in the office), lying in bed, driving, or riding along in a car, and your mind actually slowed down enough for you to take a moment to think? At that moment, you realized you did not know where you were. I am not talking about physically or geographically, but rather where you were in life.

Your mind immediately started to wander, and you began to wonder about your purpose. You ask yourself (perhaps even God), "Why am I here? What am I doing wrong? If I am doing what I am supposed to do, why do I feel so empty? Why do I feel like I am living in an alternate reality?" Many people stop there and take it no further. I adjure you to take it further. Continue to ask yourself what you are doing. Think about what is going on around you. Think about where you are spiritually. Think about whether you are chasing something that is not in God's plan for you or if you are running from what He has planned for you. You may have to ponder for some time because you may not realize it overnight. For as long as it takes, just steal away by yourself and listen for what God has to say.

So, the next time your mind slows down enough for you to question where you are, you will know exactly where you are — running to God's calling.

Tresa M. Sullivan

Time for Reflection: Encourage Yourself

Sipping Session Eleven

The Power of Repetition

One morning, I was in a rush to open the blinds. I don't know why. When I opened the first set, I could see frost on the ground, and all was still and quiet. I felt a little sad. Over the past few days, I had noticed the birds were not chirping, and the squirrels were not frolicking about as much as they do in other seasons. I stood in place for a few moments longer, thanking God for the day and all He has done.

When I plopped down in my chair and began to work, I immediately noticed the sound of a bird singing. It was as if it were saying, "Tresa, Tresa, Tresa." I was tickled. Then, I heard it again. After hearing it several more times, I finally got up to see the bird that was seemingly singing my name to me. I peered out the window but could not see the source of that beautiful sound because the sun was shining so brightly. I tried to tilt the blinds in different directions to reduce the effects of the sun's rays, but it was of no avail. I gave up and sat back down.

As the bird chirped my name again, it came to me that the chirp was a call to action. I had heard it the first time and did not move, but after several times, I got up to check out the call. In doing so, I realized it was my topic for this day: Repetition. Repetition — whether spoken, heard, read, or acted — reinforces a thought, action, or behavior, which can be a good or bad thing.

See if you can find one good thing to put in your repetition repertoire and another that you can pull out and discard. If you repeat the action enough, soon, your repertoire will be filled with good things, and there will soon be nothing to pull out to discard.

TIPs for Sips

Time for Reflection: Encourage Yourself

Sipping Session Twelve

Things I Have Learned

TIPs for Sips

I have learned that God is faithful and true, even when we are not.

I have learned that as long as I can breathe, I have a chance to get it right, make it right, and accept what is right.

I have learned that faith dictates how our story unfolds.

I have learned that love is a conscious decision.

I have learned that whoever said, "Beauty is only skin deep," does not know anything about beauty.

I have learned that it is far easier to deal with ignorance than stupidity.

I have learned that absolutely no one loves me as God does.

I have learned that forgiving others comes with healing power for myself.

I have learned that hatred and evil from others make God's love even sweeter.

I have learned that bad things happen to good people.

I have learned that there is something good to be gained, even in a bad event.

I have learned that knowledge has no value if it is not applied wisely.

Tresa M. Sullivan

I have learned to appreciate small things often taken for granted. In the end, they have more value than material things.

I have learned that vision is more than seeing what is in front of you.

I have learned that grace weighs more than gold.

I have learned that a "Jack of all trades" is a leader of none.

I have learned that mercy is a priceless jewel.

I have learned that being still is sometimes the only action I need to take.

I have learned that family is family in both good and bad times. You don't pick them; God does.

I have learned that wisdom is not wisdom if you do not share it.

I have learned that people often show you who they are, but you sometimes must put on your glasses to see it.

I have learned that the world's appetite is greater for wrong than for what is right.

I have learned that hurting someone because you can does not add a notch to your belt; it adds a scar to your heart.

I have learned that deceit is charming. Otherwise, we would not be deceived.

TIPs for Sips

I have learned that sometimes, good things look ugly.

I have learned that the truth may be ugly, but it nourishes the soul and strengthens the bones.

I have learned that my circumstances should not change my beliefs, but my beliefs should change my circumstances.

I have learned that if God is taking care of something, I should leave it alone.

I have learned that no matter how far I roam, I am still close to home and could find myself there at any moment.

I have learned that clicking my heels three times will not get me home, but God's grace will.

Time for Reflection: Encourage Yourself

Sipping Session Thirteen

Change the Light, Not the Lampshade

I was struggling with the lighting in my bedroom. One lamp was too bright, and the overhead light was too dim. I worked and reworked the positioning and even changed the lampshade. The light actually began to melt the inside of the lampshade! I thought perhaps the lampshades were made too cheaply, so I upgraded them. I changed the lightbulbs in the ceiling fan, but it never dawned on me to change the lamp's light. It was a "duh moment" when I thought to change the bulb. I was lying in bed and wondered how I could not have realized I needed to change the lightbulb.

I realized how much lightbulbs are like people. You can move the bulb from one place to another, change its covering, and even put a color wheel in front of it, but the light will always produce according to its wattage. Just the same, you can give people a good job, upgrade their wardrobe, write feel-good speeches, and provide a step-by-step guide and instructions for success, and they may put forth a colorful character for a little while and may even behave admirably. Given time, however, they will spew forth what is really inside their hearts, unless God changes them.

There's good news, though! God is in the business of changing hearts and minds, not just positions and clothes.

TIPs for Sips

Time for Reflection: Encourage Yourself

Sipping Session Fourteen

If But One

TIPs for Sips

While pondering my purpose in life and thinking of what I would like to leave behind, a few things crossed my mind:

- ❖ If I should learn but one lesson, let it be to worship God in all things, for in revering God, all else that matters is learned.
- ❖ If I should teach but one lesson, I would like it to be, "In all things, live earnestly." In living earnest, one can only reverence God, and all other growth will follow.
- ❖ If I should take but one stance, let that stance be that I will stand for the salvation of man.
- ❖ If I am grateful for but one thing, I choose grace.
- ❖ If I am thankful for but one thing, it is, indeed, mercy. But for grace and mercy, all else is in vain.
- ❖ If I should give but one remedy, let it be laughter, for as they say, "Laughter does a heart good." It is, indeed, good for the soul.
- ❖ If I should provide one single guide, may it be to walk in love. There is no greater walk than to walk in love, and there is no better reward.
- ❖ If I could effect one change, it would be to eradicate hate.
- ❖ If I should leave behind on true treasure, may that treasure be hope—hope for a better life, where there is no strain or strife. Hope gives strength to go on when all may seem lost.
- ❖ If I should discover but one single thing, may that thing be faith—faith that the hope in the revering of God provides me the fortitude to continue my stand for humanity with laughter and joy in my heart as I earnestly walk in love on the road to the true treasures of salvation—redemption, peace, and eternal bliss.

Time for Reflection: Encourage Yourself

Sipping Session Fifteen

Trees and Lichens?

As I waited for the perfect moment to capture a picture of soft yellow, golden, orange, and red leaves on a tree in my backyard, I noticed another large tree. It stretched high, with many of its leaves still green, but it was plagued with lichens (fungus). Initially, I felt sorry for the tree because I thought it was sick. I don't feel as sorry now because I have gained an understanding of its plight.

That tree is like the lives of many people. It still carries its beauty well, and its show of strength during storms is awesome. The most important thing is that the lichens are like the trials of life. The battle scars (lichens) are plainly visible, but they have not stunted the tree's growth. The lichens (troubles, sins of the past) are there for all to see, but they take nothing away from the tree itself.

Just like sin and life's troubles, they have no roots or leaves. They are a combination of fungus and algae. The algae and fungus feed each other with carbon and nitrogen, respectively. The lichen cannot live without the combination of the two—just as sin cannot survive without doubt and disobedience.

You and I are like deeply-rooted trees. Our spiritual growth and attainment of wisdom throughout life are our leaves. We have new experiences in different seasons. We learn from them as our branches grow strong, and those experiences we no longer need fall away and are replaced with new and better ones. Ailments, disbelief, and struggles are our lichens. They are only skin deep and live on the surface of our lives. Our faith, gratitude, and lessons learned add rings to our tree, and we become stronger with each experience and year. We may have to fight to weather the storm, but we rise with our arms stretched high as we glorify and thank God in all things. With each experience, our leaves return to glorious green. We can stand tall, despite the lichens.

I also understand that lichens absorb pollutants. So, let all the trash the world throws at you be like lichens. Scars will be evident, but your survival will be even more evident when the failure of life's trials is exposed because you "shall be like a tree planted by the rivers of water, that bringeth forth his fruit in his season; his leaf also shall not wither; and whatsoever he doeth shall prosper" (Psalms 13:3).

Time for Reflection: Encourage Yourself

Sipping Session Sixteen

Sometimes, You Don't Get a Second Chance

Tresa M. Sullivan

I waited all morning and well into the evening to capture the sunlight gleaming on a small tree as I had seen it the day before, but my opportunity never came. At the precise time I thought the sun would gleam on the tree and illuminate the multi-colored leaves, a cloud wisped by and stopped right in front of the sun. It just sat there for the longest, stealing away any chance I had to capture the moment for which I waited so anxiously. I was disappointed but thanked God for blessing me to have seen it when I did.

On this day, as I blankly stared out the window at that tree, I thought about how I will never in this lifetime again have the chance to capture the beautiful sight of two days ago. I may not have that chance, but God keeps right on blessing me day after day with new grace and mercy, affording me undeserved opportunities to do or say things when I get the chance — the first time.

It is up to us to learn to take advantage and do things the first time because sometimes, you don't get a second chance. We should tell our loved ones we love them every time it comes to mind, right a wrong quickly, be quick to forgive, never hesitate to do the right thing, ask for forgiveness immediately, and most importantly, never cease to pray and thank God for all things.

TIPs for Sips

Time for Reflection: Encourage Yourself

Sipping Session Seventeen

In the Woods

TIPs for Sips

Sometimes, we do not realize what we can do until we are in the midst of doing it. We do not realize how much strength and support we have until we are in a tough situation. Sometimes, we do not realize are the light for which someone is searching. As I slept one night, these words I tried to express the day before came to mind:

I did not know I was lost in the woods until I realized I was in the woods. I did not know I could survive being lost in the woods until I realized I was already surviving. When I realized I was in the woods, I was in my house. It was I who provided light in the house. I may not be able to chop down the cedars of Lebanon, but I have a Father who can. Not only can He chop them down, but He can also build a house from them just for me. Not only can He build me a house, but He can also have a mansion made.

My friend, the next time you are lost and wandering in the woods, look for the light. My Father has given me a light to share. He let me know that I cannot lead anyone through the woods if I have not hewn a path myself. While I am not begging for the struggle, I am taking things as they come — the bad with the good, the sunshine and the rain.

I am not trying to walk in someone else's shoes; I am offering a pair of mine — a pair that has already been broken in and is comfortable. They may not be an exact fit, but they may prevent some of the bleeding caused by thorns in the woods.

People who know me know I do not like screaming and shouting, but pardon me for a moment. Allow me to be Walter White[a]:

Tresa M. Sullivan

"If the Lord blesses, I am going to shout on this one!"

I just cannot keep it to myself. It is bubbling up in my soul, tingling in my fingers, flowing down my eyes, and lifting my heart!

Yes, I am in the woods, but it is good in the woods. Pain and strain are in the woods. There is healing in the woods. Joy and laughter are in the woods. Grace and mercy are in the woods. Peace and comfort are in the woods. Love and hope are in the woods. Praying never ceases in the woods.

A lot is going on in the woods. Come, let us make a neighborhood in the woods, for God Almighty is in the woods!

TIPs for Sips

Time for Reflection: Encourage Yourself

Tresa M. Sullivan

Sipping Session Eighteen

To Dine with Danger

TIPs for Sips

Two young men and a young lady were asked to join an older man of eloquent verse to dine at an elegant restaurant. Their first thought was to decline, but he spoke so enticingly, they accepted his invite.

The man lavished them with drink and wine, and the food was so divine. One young man had little to drink because he wanted to think. The other dived right in. The young lady had her fair share but did so cautiously.

The man told them, "Take a look around at how I entertain among the famed. Join my team, get in the game, and for you, I will do the same." He promised to shower them with diamonds, pearls, and gold. All they had to do was exactly as they were told.

When the entrees were served, the young man who wasn't drinking remarked, "Wow, that's too much gravy," and pushed his plate aside.

The elderly man asked, all puffed up with pride, "What, you don't eat swine?"

The young man replied, "It is not the swine that bothers me; it's the lying. You've been talking since we got here and sat down at the table. I think we should leave now while we are still able."

Taken aback, the old man cracked, "Nothing I've promised is fabled."

"Ah, but you failed to say how arduous it will be. Neither did you say—when you promised fame, riches, and gold—that it would only cost our souls."

As the young man walked out with the young lady close behind, the older man opened his mouth to shout. Instead, when he saw the second young man was too busy gulping to notice, he opened so wide, you could see fire in his hollow. He gulped the young man down with one fatal swallow.

Wherever you go, make sure you know with whom you entertain and dine. Should they be the unsavory kind, don't even sit for the wine.

TIPs for Sips

Time for Reflection: Encourage Yourself

Sipping Session Nineteen

I Don't Know His Name

TIPs for Sips

I love someone who loves me more, and I don't know His name. He loves me more than I love myself or I ever could. In this love, there is no shame, but I don't know His name.

Some call Him Yahweh; others say El Shaddai. Some call Him Qanna; others say Adonai. El Elyon, El Olam, Elohim, and the many variations of "Jehovah" are all descriptive of God, but are any truly His name? It doesn't matter to me because I love Him just the same.

He wakes me every morning and watches me when I sleep. With every breath I take, I know my soul is His to keep. He is my shepherd and I, His lamb, but I don't know His name. He guides me and gently nudges me in line when I have gone astray. He provides my every need and has planned my future. It's one that's brightly lit. I am forever grateful. With my voice, I will give Him praise. In blind faith, I will follow wherever He may lead. I am most confident in His every lead, and though I still don't know His name, I think I'll call Him Father and love Him just the same.

He says, "I Am Alpha and Omega; I AM THAT I AM."

Since I Am is who He is, that is perfectly fine, because it is NOT important that I know His name, but that He knows mine.

Tresa M. Sullivan

Time for Reflection: Encourage Yourself

Sipping Session Twenty

Rise and Shine

Good Morning! Rise and shine, knowing that God has given you the strength to persevere. Whatever your circumstances may be today, you have got it covered. If that means getting on your hands and knees, or sinking your teeth into a problem and spitting it out, or putting your foot on the devil's head, you can do it.

You may have to reach out and ask for help, but you have got it. Your help may already be on the way. Someone may already be praying for you. You may get an unexpected call from a source of strength. And, of course, there is nothing between you and God except a prayer. You can always tag Him into the match.

So, let's get at it. May God's favor shine upon you as brightly as the sun, and may your blessings be as innumerable as the stars.

TIPs for Sips

Time for Reflection: Encourage Yourself

Sipping Session Twenty-One

Sort Your Friends

TIPs for Sips

Sort your friends, company, and associates like you sort your mail and laundry. If someone is bringing junk to you, don't allow them to cross your threshold. Get rid of the junk!

When you get a piece of junk mail, you often take one glance at it and know it can be thrown away. Another time, you may come across something and say, "I cannot use this, but someone else can," so you recycle it. If you pay that kind of attention to your mail, don't you think it is just as important to sort your acquaintances?

If a person is constantly bringing negative information and vibes to you, shut that down. Messy Misery loves company, and that is the kind of company you cannot afford to keep. If Alice is too clingy and needy, and you know that Joyce loves attention, recycle your relationship with both of them by introducing them to one another. Let them fill the void each has within.

Now, don't get me wrong: I am not saying do not be kind and do not help people in need. Instead, I suggest sorting those relationships like you sort your laundry. Every load has a temperature setting of its own, and when you mix the darks with the lights, they sometimes bleed. If you are tired of being bled on, sort it right. It only takes a few washes to get it right.

When you come across that piece of laundry without a tag, and you know not what to do with it, you test the fabric. If it is cheap, you know it will not last, so don't waste your time trying to take care of a pair of see-through 'wish' pants. Just throw them away. Yes, you may have spent a few dollars on them, but you don't want to spend more taking care of them than you paid for them—and you still cannot wear them.

So, the next time Sneaky Shenita just happens to drop by because she thought she saw Messy Melinda with Cheating Charlie, tell her you cannot talk today or any other day because you are busy sorting things out.

True and sincere relationships can be ironed with the linen setting. If the relationship burns a hole and becomes see-through on the synthetic setting, that is exactly what it is: an imitation. Let it go and forget it.

Time for Reflection: Encourage Yourself

Sipping Session Twenty-Two

Courage

Start today knowing there is a difference between having the courage to do things and a willingness to do something foolish.

Be courageous when the situation warrants it and know when jumping all in is a foolish thing to do. Courage enables us to resist what may be the popular thing to do when it costs our integrity. Courage fuels our will to do what is proper, even if it results in the loss of some material things, superficial friends, or some form of power. Upon such losses, those things should be reevaluated to determine their actual value.

Are they worth your peace of mind? Are they worth your soul?

When you make a choice of your own volition, and your conviction tells you it is right, have the courage to do the right thing. If you lose anything by doing the right thing, I guarantee the things you lose will be far outweighed by the things you gain or the things that remain.

Time for Reflection: Encourage Yourself

Sipping Session Twenty-Three

Problems

Thank God for another day and another opportunity to be pleasing in His sight!

Problems. What is a problem? A problem is another opportunity to be pleasing in God's sight, and we can benefit from that. So, call a problem what it is: a problem! Then, call upon what God has given you to overcome and solve it. Use the resources He has provided, whether that is prayer, faith, your phone-a-friend option, or all of the above. The good thing about it is that you never run out of those things!

You can phone a friend. That includes Jesus! You know He "is on the mainline — tell Him what you want"[b] as many times as you need to.

You can whisper a prayer in your heart without ever opening your mouth. Praise God!

Your faith is with you always, growing stronger with each problem. Just reflect a moment. How many times has He not brought you out? You ought to look at your problems now, then look at God just waiting for you to "use what you got."

TIPs for Sips

Time for Reflection: Encourage Yourself

Tresa M. Sullivan

Sipping Session Twenty-Four

With You

"When you pass through the waters, I will be with you." (Isaiah 43:2)

When you are going through adversity, difficulties, or suffering loss, you don't have to worry about going under. You don't have to worry about getting to the other side.

When you have done all that you can and are at your weakest, if you just believe, look up, and lift your heart and voice to God, you don't have to worry.

Even if your boat sinks, you can float. If you keep your eyes on the prize, you can walk out on the water.

Our Heavenly Father has you when all else fails. He had you from the start.

Tresa M. Sullivan

Time for Reflection: Encourage Yourself

Sipping Session Twenty-Five

Riches

Riches. What is it truly? Have you ever spent too much on an item, only to find you never use it or lose it? Have you gone to trade it in (such as a vehicle), only to find its value has depreciated greatly? It is then when you realize it really wasn't that valuable at all. You may have spent a pretty penny for it, but that thing did not add value to your life.

Let us busy ourselves this day working for something that will never tarnish…something that has already been secured and cannot be lost or stolen. It will never depreciate and has already been paid in full.

To what am I referring? What is this thing of value?

SALVATION.

It has been paid for with the ultimate price: the precious life of the Son of God Almighty and is the most valuable gift of all time. All we have to do is accept it.

Time for Reflection: Encourage Yourself

Tresa M. Sullivan

Sipping Session Twenty-Six

Footstool

Psalms 110:1 reads, "The LORD said unto my Lord, 'Sit thou at My right hand, until I make thine enemies thy footstool.'" Wow! How rich and grand is that?

I pray you know that as an heir to the Kingdom, He will make thine enemies your footstool as well. However, you must read, acknowledge, understand, heed, and act accordingly. Be obedient. Do what the LORD said. He said, "Sit thou at My right hand." He did not say, "Jump up and down, run around, and scream." He did not say, "Take up thy sword." He did not say, "Use a vile tongue." He did not say, "Set your trap." He said, "SIT" — meaning "BE STILL." Where did He say to sit? "At My right hand." You know what it means to be the right-hand man, right? Simply put, it is an Indispensable Helper. Now, that is not your job; that belongs to Jesus — but a right-hand man is also a Chief Helper, and that is you.

Let's now take a closer look at what the LORD said. "Sit thou at my right hand." That means you must be performing what is required of you to earn that title. You must live righteously to be a Chief Helper. If you are doing your part as a Chief Helper, you are doing what God asks of you — not what He asks of Jesus, me, or anyone else. It is what He asks of you specifically. When you are doing that, then all you have to do is wait. He will, indeed, make your enemies your footstool.

Like the walls of Jericho, your enemy's plans for you will come tumbling down. You will find yourself at peace in the middle of the storm. Do your due diligence and see how foolishness rolls off your mind like water on a duck's back. How are you going to rest your feet if you are not in your seat? Now, sit down! For the Lord God said, "Be still, and know that I am God" (Psalms 46:10).

Tresa M. Sullivan

Time for Reflection: Encourage Yourself

Sipping Session Twenty-Seven

For a Limited Time Only

Ooowee! You had better hurry! The limited-time-only sale will not be around forever! The wool is going quickly.

You know as well as I do that if anyone is rushing you to buy today, you need to turn and move swiftly in the other direction. Why? For one thing, you can bet the sale will come around again. Another reason is the proverbial, "If it sounds too good to be true, it is probably too good to be true."

The only thing that is truly once-in-a-lifetime and truly for a limited time only that is free and too good to be true is salvation—and it has already been purchased just for you. No one can talk you in or out of salvation. No one can live for you and exact your fate except you. Your soul's salvation has already been paid for, and it doesn't cost you a thing.

However, it does come with instructions, warnings, and directions, and you must use as directed. If you don't use as directed, the most serious side effects are death and Hell. Don't be fooled by the limited-time-only generic brand sales. In this case, only the brand name will do.

WARNING: The Creator of the universe warns against buying into generic ideologies. Sin IS dangerous to your health and soul, and once your prescription expires, it is expired. So, read your Bible, act as directed, and follow-up with the prescriber often.

Time for Reflection: Encourage Yourself

Sipping Session Twenty-Eight

Ticket for Nothing and the Ride Is Free

TIPs for Sips

How many times have you heard, "Nothing is free"? Probably as many times as you have heard, "The best things in life are free." How can it be both ways? Now, there's a paradox for you!

How can nothing be free when the best things in life are free?

Well, let me explain from my vantage point.

The two greatest gifts of all time ARE free: Salvation and love. One (salvation) was purchased with the ultimate price—the life of the greatest Prince in all creation. The other (unconditional love), He and His Father provide at no cost to you. There is no way you can pay for either.

So, what is the price you pay? The exercising of faith, the demonstration of love, and the exhibition of righteous works! Think of Heaven as your destination. The tickets cost nothing, and the ride is free.

Hold on a second, though: I don't want you to skate off thinking the ride will always be smooth. There may be some strong winds and turbulence, but the landing is always perfect.

I have my ticket, and I am working on my ride. How about you?

Time for Reflection: Encourage Yourself

Sipping Session Twenty-Nine

What Are You Wearing Today?

Every day when getting dressed, some of us add accessories to make ourselves look good…or so we think. I submit to you a new routine.

How about today, instead of putting on lipstick, you try a coat of "watch your mouth" and "truthfulness." Instead of stretching out your hands for nail polish and rings, stretch them out to help someone. Before you slip on that pair of pumps or stilettos, slip on a comfortable pair of feet that are not swift to run to mischief. Forego the eyeshadow and replace it with a coat of "overlooking foolishness." Instead of applying foundation, apply a coat of the Word to prepare you for the day. Skip the blush and add a stroke of warm-heartedness. There is no need for eyeliner if you line it all up with a little love and goodwill. Leave that wig on the stand and slap on some "mindfulness" and "thoughtfulness."

Then, when you are all done with the new routine, step back and look at yourself in the mirror. It may take some time getting used to it, but it sure looks good on you!

TIPs for Sips

Time for Reflection: Encourage Yourself

Sipping Session Thirty

I Choose to Live in the Woods

TIPs for Sips

Sam Walter Foss[c] wrote the poem "The House by the Side of the Road." He wanted to be a friend to man. I suppose he wished to entertain passersby, provide a forgotten item, or even a drink of water.

That is not my desire. I choose to live in the woods, away from the fray. I am not here for the man on the road, for he usually knows the direction in which he chose to travel. Leave me in the woods for those who have lost their way.

May I forever be able to direct them back to the road and assure them all is not lost. May I provide nourishment for the soul and a light to the road. May my voice bring calmness to a troubled heart, and my words uplift the downtrodden.

Yes, let me live deep in the woods, where the path is overgrown.

May I hew, along with the forlorn, a new path to the road where God's everlasting light is ever shown.

Time for Reflection: Encourage Yourself

Sipping Session Thirty-One

Voices and Words

On this day, I woke up with two words on my mind. While they should have been, "Thank God," they were, instead, 'voices and words.' They were quickly replaced with "Thank You, God! Thank You, Jesus!"

Still, my mind kept reverting to 'voice and words.' For a few minutes, I could not figure out why. Then, it struck me: We all hear voices in our heads/minds. They are the voices of our consciousness, wisdom, and guidance from the Holy Spirit. They are also the voices of derailment from evil principalities. The voices give us words for action or direction. The words we choose to perform in our behaviors determine who we are.

Let's take a look at some of the action words we may find ourselves in conflict with each day:

1. Forget or regret: Do we choose to forget actions or behaviors that are irrelevant and really do not make a difference in our lives, or do we take action and say or do something that we later regret?
2. Revenge or avenge: Do we get revenge for something someone has said or done to us, or do we let God avenge our mistreatment?
3. Strike out or back out: Do we strike out at others when we are hurt or do we back out of foolishness? Backing out of foolishness does not mean to back down from what you believe. It means saying or taking appropriate actions without becoming entangled in bad behaviors.
4. Step up or step down: Do we step up in times of need for our family, friends, and others we can help, or do we step down, remove ourselves, and let others figure it out the best way they can?

5. Step in or step out: Do we step in and do the right thing when we see things are going wrong or being handled inappropriately, or do we step out of the picture and let it slide?
6. Tango or solo: Do we fight in unnecessary circumstances, or do we take the high road and go it solo?
7. Shout out or shoutout: Do we yell and scream at every single thing others do wrong or not pleasing to us, or do we let small things go and remember to give a shoutout to others when they do something good or go out of their way to do something for you or others?
8. Show out or show up: Do we act a fool when things are not going our way, or do we show we can be the bigger person, think things through, and try to work it out? Do we show up with plausible, potential ideas, remedies, and solutions?
9. Throw down or slow down (hold it down): Do we fight first and think later, or do we slow it down, think through things, and take actions to hold down the family, even if that is painful sometimes?
10. Blow up or grow up: Do we explode when we are unhappy, or do we refrain from bad behaviors and give ourselves time to handle bad situations appropriately?
11. Deflect or reflect: Do we deflect and blame our behaviors on others or bring up things others have done to distract from our behaviors, or do we take time to think about mistakes we make and have empathy for others?
12. Sit in or fit in/jump in: Do we find ourselves being there but not participating in important things, or do we behave like a family member and fit in and jump in to do whatever is necessary to make things right?

13. Relate or berate: Do we relate and empathize with others who make mistakes, knowing that we, too, have made many, or do we berate them, crushing their hearts and souls?
14. Escalate or deescalate: Are we quick to fan the flames in a bad situation, or do we quickly try to calm one another and resolve things with level heads?
15. Discover or recover: Do we discover the root of problems and proactively seek solutions, or do we find ourselves recovering from the results/consequences of behaviors and actions for which we ignored?
16. Defend or amend/mend: Do we defend taking offensive actions, or do we amend to make minor changes to keep the harmony or mend and repair relationships that are too valuable to allow human error to destroy them?
17. Ride out or ride it out: When things get really tough, do we roll out and leave, or do we ride out the storm and arise victoriously?
18. Drown or crown: Do we drown ourselves in the sorrows and cares of this world, or do we face the problems, draw upon our faith, and use the strength, help, and people God has provided and obtain our crown in the end?
19. Elevate or depreciate: Do we lift ourselves by lifting others, or do we find ourselves down low because we are constantly tearing down others, hoping to reduce or eliminate their self-esteem or faith and discourage them?
20. Alive or living: Are we merely alive, going through daily routines and rituals, or are we living examples of the Christ within us?
21. Sin or win: Do we sin by exercising negative words, or do we win by exercising positive words and being a blessing to ourselves and others?

22. Ascend or descend: After we have decided which action words to exercise, we will either ascend to be with the Heavenly Father or descend and remain forever with evil principalities.

Tresa M. Sullivan

Time for Reflection: Encourage Yourself

Sipping Session Thirty-Two

Water My Soul

Believe it or not, I am a nature lover. I love admiring God's art. He is sovereign and omnipotent. His skills transcend the imagination, and His art is faultless and flawless.

When I look at the dry earth and grass and think how some people may think there is no hope for it, I think about how just a refreshing rain can rejuvenate and restore them to their natural appearance in almost no time at all.

I, too, am among God's beings of nature. I am a work of art. As the earth needs water, so do I. I need water physically and spiritually. I drink natural water for my body to survive, and I absorb God's Word as water for my soul.

I pray God waters my soul daily so that my actions and words show the vitality, love, and truth that God has bestowed upon me. I pray my soul is watered enough to irrigate all who cross my path.

Time for Reflection: Encourage Yourself

Tresa M. Sullivan

Sipping Session Thirty-Three

Value Added

Years ago, when businesses started throwing around the term "Value Added," it referred to the increase in value at each stage of production after initial costs. Over the years, it has also come to mean extra features that a person is willing to pay to have, as well as something considered to improve something or someone by its purchase.

In this life, most of us have two jobs: a natural job and a spiritual job. On occasion, I think about the things I purchase with the earnings from my natural job: home, cars, jewelry, things for the house, things for the guys, and a few gifts here and there. Sometimes, I stop and wonder if any of those things really add value to my life (some do, some do not). Then, I give a few things away, thinking they may add value to someone else's life (maybe it does, maybe it doesn't). In either case, I am sure I could live without a lot of the things I purchase with my natural income.

As I get older, I think more and more about my spiritual job. I know I cannot earn what I hope will be my dividend, but I hope my appraisal/performance evaluation shows the value added to my soul. I pray that what I give in the natural through my spiritual job can help someone — anyone — add value to their soul.

The next time you make a purchase, stop for a moment and think about whether or not it is "Value Added."

Tresa M. Sullivan

Time for Reflection: Encourage Yourself

Sipping Session Thirty-Four

Faith Conquers Fear

Our faith should conquer our fears. There is never a moment when God takes you somewhere where He cannot protect you. We are always safe and protected in His care, even when bad things happen. When we are in His will, even the result of bad things lands a righteous soul in Heaven. It is when we step out of His will and His way that we begin to falter.

Make no mistake: There is a difference between falter and suffer. We will all suffer to some extent in this life. Unpleasantness introduces itself to us early in life, and to suffer for Christ's sake is truly a joy. However, when we falter, we lose our momentum and become weak. That is because we have not found our way spiritually…or we have lost our way.

Fortunately for us, God is always there to gently guide us back to the right path — if we let Him. For some, it shows up as tough love, but it is love, nonetheless.

When you truly believe you are directed by God, move forward. His safety net is always there, just in case you make a mistake. God is with you, so those who are against you can forget it!

Move out in faith, conquer fear, and crush it in its tracks!

Time for Reflection: Encourage Yourself

Sipping Session Thirty-Five

What Are You Chasing?

Have you ever awakened and asked yourself, "Why am I here? What am I supposed to be doing?" You feel like there is something special you should be doing and know there is more for you to do, so you start a new journey. You begin planning what you can do to make a difference.

Once you get started, you feel really good about what you are doing until you wake up one day and again ask yourself, "Why am I here?"

Some people are paper chasers. Others chase fame. Some people chase the wind. Others chase dreams. Some people chase a feeling. Others chase people. All of them eventually find themselves asking the same questions and wonder why they are not fulfilled.

People are not fulfilled because they chase the wrong things.

"But seek ye first the Kingdom of God, and His righteousness; and all these things shall be added unto you."
(Matthew 6:33)

What are you chasing?

Tresa M. Sullivan

Time for Reflection: Encourage Yourself

Sipping Session Thirty-Six

The Name "Jesus"

Tresa M. Sullivan

When I hear the song, "Something About the Name Jesus,"[d] it almost doesn't matter who is singing it, it gets down in my soul. As my son often says, "That hit the soul."

Have you ever been sick or downtrodden and just said His name? Have you ever been stuck not knowing what to do, or afraid and just called His name?

Well, I have. If you haven't done so in trying times, you should try it. If you have ever called on the name of Jesus in times of trouble, you know you can call on Him anytime. You know that it is not just a name you call when you are happy, as it becomes the first word that comes to mind when things aren't going well, as well as when things are as right as rain. You know the power of the name. You know that it is real. You know you can call Him, and everything will be alright.

He is the only one who can make it right in the time of storms, in the time of trouble, or in the time of pain. Call on Him and know deep down in your soul that everything is going to be alright.

Things may not always work out the way you want, but they will always work. If you don't believe me, try it. Call on Jesus when you are happy, sad, mad, or confused. Call on Jesus when you are by yourself or standing strong in a crowd. You will see He will be there for you, just like He is always there for me.

Then, after you have taken notice of how often He is there for you, let me know if it is not, indeed, the sweetest name you know. Praise God!

TIPs for Sips

Time for Reflection: Encourage Yourself

Tresa M. Sullivan

Sipping Session Thirty-Seven

Be Kind

When God asks us to love one another, He is not asking us to do something impossible or even something we would not want for ourselves. He is not asking us to abandon all common sense and recklessly go out of our way for strangers or even those with whom we share a common affection. He asks us to be benevolent people, a people known for goodwill and expressions of kindness.

What harm does it do for you to be kind? Hebrews 13:2 reads, "Be not forgetful to entertain strangers: for thereby, some have entertained angels unawares." Listen when requests are made of you. Pay attention to people. If you see a place to help and you can afford to do so, do it.

God has provided for you…and He always will.

Time for Reflection: Encourage Yourself

Sipping Session Thirty-Eight

'No' is Not a Bad Word

Let's explore times when you should say "No."

Many of us give of ourselves and possessions freely. We give of our resources tirelessly, often with no respite in sight. It is only when we are worn and drained that we realize we are doing too much.

I often remind people that time is the greatest gift we can give. It is also one of our most valuable resources. Time is irretrievable. It should be respected and used wisely. People sometimes think if they use your time instead of a tangible resource (i.e., money, objects, food, etc.) that somehow, they are not using or taking advantage of you. That is a misconception by both them and you, and you are within your rights to say no.

"No" is not a bad word. It is okay to say no. The reason may be the same reason God tells us no: It may not be the best time, especially when saying yes could yield a negative consequence. It may also not be in your best interest. It is perfectly fine to say no when you have too much on your plate, you are unprepared, the request is not something you are comfortable with, or you are not good at performing the request. You may even say no when you need restoration yourself.

In any case, before you say yes to the next request, take time to consider your own circumstances. Feel okay about saying no if it is not the best thing to do. If saying no causes a rift in the relationship, perhaps the relationship is not what you thought it was.

TIPs for Sips

Time for Reflection: Encourage Yourself

Tresa M. Sullivan

Sipping Session Thirty-Nine

Let Wisdom Be Your Defense

TIPs for Sips

"If any of you lack wisdom, let him as of God, that giveth to all men liberally, and upbraideth not; and it shall be given him." (James 1:5)

I find myself often asking God to give me wisdom, knowledge, understanding, and the ability to apply them daily. If you feel like you need wisdom, ask God. However, in doing so, remember not to ask for something and not use it. If you ask Him for something, be ready for it. Be prepared to use what is given to you, or it may be taken away (you may also lose other blessings and gifts in the process). If you do not understand something, ask Him. He has blessed us with two precious gifts that enable us to contact Him without miscommunication: Jesus and the Holy Ghost. All you need to do is ask. You don't have to ask for it over and over, as I can guarantee you: He heard you the first time. From the time you ask, start thanking Him. It will either come in time, or it is something you do not need.

I want to caution you: Be careful what you ask for. If you keep begging for something, He just may grant your desire, and you then discover it was not what you needed at all because it only made things worse.

So, before you ask, first seek wisdom, knowledge, and application. Let wisdom be your defense against the cares of this world. Let its application be your goal. Sometimes, you may not be pleased with the application, but you will be playing DEFENSE. In this life, defense is your best offense.

Time for Reflection: Encourage Yourself

Sipping Session Forty

Doesn't Cost You Anything

Have you ever noticed the things that make you the happiest cost $0.00? I am sure you have heard the saying, "The best things in life are free" or "Money can't buy me love." That is because those are among the things you cannot buy: joy, happiness, love, peace, freedom of choice, and life ever after.

Now, there are times when you pay the consequence for choices or decisions you make, but it cannot go unnoticed that the opportunity to make that choice is free. We have free will to decide how we will spend eternity. We can place value on worldly things, but you know as well as I do, those things perish. It may not always be easy to do the right thing, but I guarantee it will be well worth it.

The life God has promised us, Jesus has provided us, and the Holy Ghost guides us to has been purchased with the ultimate price, and it did not cost you anything. Earthly struggles and challenges are your opportunities to exercise the free things in life. Sometimes, they may be tough, but you never have to go it alone. The love, peace, happiness, and joy you experience after a struggle are enjoyed so much more when you do the right thing. There is absolutely no comparison to the eternal bliss that awaits those who serve and love the Lord!

Time for Reflection: Encourage Yourself

Sipping Session Forty-One

Don't Let Denomination Become Abomination

There are some things to which I neither conform, appreciate, nor tolerate. Among those things are disrespect, liars, self-righteousness, religio-centrism (religious exclusivism), and disingenuous or insincere people. I will not tackle them all, but I will speak on religious exclusivism, as it has permeated the faith of far too many people.

There is but one God. No matter what you call Him, He is God Almighty. He has cautioned use about being self-righteous, and that includes religious exclusivism. We have taken our belief to a level such that we don't take the time to talk about Jesus and show charity/love in all we do. We are far too busy denouncing denominations to proclaim our Lord and Savior as we should.

Religious exclusivism is another slick trick of Satan. He divides and conquers by using the very thing that saves us (our belief in Christ Jesus) to create an abomination in God's sight.

The Gospel brings salvation to all, but we have to love as Jesus loves. We have the power to stop Satan in his tracks. We do not have to allow him to drive a wedge between us and our fellow brothers and sisters.

Let us be the ones to denounce denominations and proclaim salvation.

Tresa M. Sullivan

Time for Reflection: Encourage Yourself

Sipping Session Forty-Two

Tame or Flame

"And the tongue is a fire, a world of iniquity; so is the tongue among our members, that it defileth the whole body, and setteth on fire the course of nature; and it is set on fire of Hell." (James 3:6)

Why is it that we can discipline our children, train our pets, guide a 3,000-pound car easily, develop a habit, carry out rituals, and even train our bodies, but yet we cannot manage to keep our mouths in line? We may start with good intentions but somehow find ourselves in trouble. My friend, that should not be so. You cannot "let the thing under your nose get the thing under your clothes" caught in Hell's fire. I realize it is not an easy thing to do, but we must hold our peace when prudent to do so.

"Even a fool, when he holdeth his peace, is counted wise: and he that shutteth his lips is esteemed a man of understanding." (Proverbs 17:28)

To speak in jest is okay, as long as you are not hurtful with what you say. Should you discover your words harmful, be quick to seek forgiveness. The same goes for intentional harsh words. There is absolutely nothing that has to be said harshly. Nothing. Soft and thoughtful words bear as much weight as harsh ones.

Taming the tongue does not just refer to refraining from saying hurtful things; it also applies to speaking up and doing so truthfully in situations that warrant discussion. Take time to assess the conversation and situation, then speak (or not speak). If you don't tame it up, in the end, God will flame it up. Go in peace.

Time for Reflection: Encourage Yourself

Tresa M. Sullivan

Sipping Session Forty-Three

Love Deeply

As a child and young adult, I was a little bold, outspoken, and frank. It was not meant to be hurtful, as my desire was only to be helpful.

Over time, I realized I could use kind words to say many of the same things I once said boldly with words that may have been harsh. Some may say I have grown soft. I prefer to think I now just love deeply.

I learned to talk about behavior, not the person. I learned how to express disappointment in their action, not the person. Time has taught me that a sharp tongue can cut a person to the core — potentially to the point of no return. I understand that nurturing and not nagging bring about change. I know how to be firm in what I say, yet be kind. I have learned that firm words followed by true compassion and a gentle smile tend to condemn the behavior and show a deep love and respect for those I care about. I have learned that I never know what is going on in people's minds and that what I say could make or break them. I, for one, would much rather make than break someone. I realized if consideration is what I want from others, I must be considerate.

So, the next time you are disappointed in a person's behavior, try a few words of compassion.

"Blessed are the merciful; for they shall obtain mercy."
(Matthew 5:7)

Tresa M. Sullivan

Time for Reflection: Encourage Yourself

Sipping Session Forty-Four

The Light Within

Have you ever noticed how much attention people pay to athletes, actors, music artists, rich people, and spiritual and political leaders? Our children mimic their behaviors, and we even find ourselves sometimes repeating something we heard them say. People, at large, are on their bandwagon and give credence to their beliefs and ideas until they do something that really crosses the line. Then, the "star" quickly falls from grace. The general public becomes disappointed and is quick to let each other know. The shame in that is this: The "star" should have never been counted on as a pillar of society. They are ordinary people living under different circumstances.

Each of us has the light within ourselves to be an example for our children and community. We should let our light so shine that others will see Jesus in us and be drawn unto God.

Stop looking to someone else to be the beacon. Take a stand. The absolute worst thing that could ever happen is that you go to Hell following someone else's lead.

Time for Reflection: Encourage Yourself

Tresa M. Sullivan

Sipping Session Forty-Five

Games

On many board games, there are often places on the board where you get stuck, and someone comes along to send you back to where you started.

In the game of life, there are spots where you get stuck. It is so frustrating, but you do not have to start all over again. In this life, even if you make the wrong move and get stuck, God does not send you back to the beginning. You just have to listen and take heed to His Word. Then, you have to keep moving along the path. You cannot lie down and wallow where you falter. You must tuck the lesson away in your heart and head, not allowing the mistake to consume you.

Even when you are playing the board game, you never remember where you got kicked off the board and sent back to start, so never let the place where you falter in life be known as the place people see you wallow. Let it be known as the place where you started the good journey because the only time you get kicked out of the game of life (no pun intended) is when you become a bedfellow with Lucifer. Not only will you lose your turn, but you also lose your soul.

Tresa M. Sullivan

Time for Reflection: Encourage Yourself

Sipping Session Forty-Six

Take Time to Pay Attention

One particular Wednesday, I was in total bewilderment when I realized Thursday was not going to be Friday. My mom and I had just talked about the month being half-gone. It amazes me how days seem so long while working, but at the very same time, it seems as though the world and time are whizzing by — something that is not realized until we actually slow down to take a look.

The paradox is that we work long hours, which makes time seem to move slowly, yet we miss out on so much life, which makes time seem to move quickly around us. Let us not be so consumed with our daily work and chores that we fail to remember the grace and mercy of God, because the natural things for which we are working are all vanity and shall pass away.

Let our fervent prayers and work be for a higher goal. Let us take time here on earth to appreciate our natural blessings: our families, friends, and nature. We should pay attention to our bodies and souls as well. They, too, are God's works of art. Tomorrow is not promised, so find something in God's art studio (it should not be hard to do) to relax your mind and refresh your soul.

TIPs for Sips

Time for Reflection: Encourage Yourself

Tresa M. Sullivan

Sipping Session Forty-Seven

What's on Your Thirds?

TIPs for Sips

When I was growing up, we had a little slang saying we used: "What's on your thirds?" It was in no way formal English, but we knew what we were being asked: What are your plans for the day? The question may not have required much thought from many of us, but it did require some thought from me.

What's on my thirds? I had to think about it.

My firsts were to do whatever chores my parents required of me. My seconds were whatever tasks I had for school. My thirds were the things I wanted to do, provided I had time to do them before it was time for me to prepare for bed.

As an adult (okay…I cannot deny it any longer: I am considered an adult), my thirds have changed. They changed with my priorities and are above and beyond my previous count.

Today, my firsts are focusing on what my Heavenly Father would have me to do. My seconds are things that are required and expected of me as a wife and mother. My thirds are to make what is on my firsts be what is on my thirds. I now have fourths and fifths. My fourths are things that take care of my mind, body, and soul. My fifths are things that I would like to do as entertainment.

I respectfully ask you: What's on your thirds…or fifths?

Tresa M. Sullivan

Time for Reflection: Encourage Yourself

Sipping Session Forty-Eight

Your Survival Kit

Tresa M. Sullivan

The universe is a gigantic place. Earth is but a speck within; an ocean is even smaller. Yet, if you were in the center of an ocean, it would seem as large as the world. Without help, regardless of your swimming skills, you can expect to drown.

In this life, think of yourself as being in the center of an ocean. You are surrounded by the dangerous sharks of life (enemies, temptations, your fears, loneliness, greed, and dishonesty, just to name a few). How do you survive in the middle of an ocean? With a lifejacket. It is absolutely amazing how something as small as a lifejacket can keep you afloat in a vast ocean.

God has provided you a lifejacket, which is prayer. You do know, however, that staying afloat will not keep you alive, right? You still need food and fresh water, so the Keeper of the universe gives you more. The Word is your bread. It keeps you nourished (mind, body, and soul). The Holy Spirit is your water. It keeps you hydrated and revived. The Holy Spirit guides you toward land, pulling you away from danger. It gives you the weapons such as faith, godly works, peace, joy, love, humility, meekness, grace, and mercy to ward off dangers of the world.

Your survival kit is packed to the brim with soul-saving tools. Don't drown unnecessarily. God provided you a lifejacket. Put it on and use it.

"Pray without ceasing."
(1 Thessalonians 5:17)

TIPs for Sips

Time for Reflection: Encourage Yourself

Tresa M. Sullivan

Sipping Session Forty-Nine

You Are the Lifeline

TIPs for Sips

Now that you have been pulled to safety and are no longer gasping for air in the ocean, it is your turn to come to the rescue of others. Do not leave anyone flailing.

When you see someone struggling, do not hesitate to help if you can. Throw out the lifeline and reel them in to safety. It is your obligation to do so.

You have weathered the storm and raging winds—and you have the scars to prove it. You are now the lighthouse. What good is the light if it is covered and others cannot see it?

You are a living testimony. Leave on the light, grab your vest and survival kit, and head toward the ocean. Get in your boat because it is now your job to save the next person afloat.

Tresa M. Sullivan

Time for Reflection: Encourage Yourself

Sipping Session Fifty

Treat Your Soul Like You Treat Your Hair, Not Your Nails

TIPs for Sips

This thought may not be for everyone. In fact, only half of it is for me.

Have you ever gone to the salon, gotten your hair done, and thought to yourself, "Hmm… I could have done that myself!"? I know I have and, on occasion, did not pay for the service. It is a waste of time and money to go to the hairdresser for an expensive style that will last one day — or two, at the most. You want your hair to look great and be healthy and manageable once you leave the salon. I cannot speak for you, but I know I have left a salon and said to myself, "I will not go there again." In all honesty, I have even said, "Maybe I will give her two more strikes." That's right. I said it. In order to get healthy hair, you cannot go one time and expect a miracle.

If you put that much thought into your hair, why not put at least as much thought into your soul? Every day, you are doing something to make sure your hair is the way you want it, even if it is only tying it down or putting on a bonnet. Treat your soul the same way you treat your hair.

When you enter into a church, a Christian relationship, or any relationship, give it time to see if it will nourish you from the inside. Make sure your soul is not only looking good on the outside but is also well on the inside. If the church or relationship is not fortifying your soul, let it go. Of course, you have to study to show yourself approved unto God and hone your ability to separate the good from the bad. Just think: You cannot expect the hairdresser to conduct the daily maintenance of your hair, right? If there is a hailstorm and you must go outside, you put on a raincoat to protect your body…and hair. Just the same, if it is a hell storm all around, make sure you put on your soul gear: the word of armor, the shield of faith, and thigh-high boots of good works.

Don't treat your soul like you treat your nails. I simply cannot go to the salon and pay money for someone to sand down my nails to the skin of my nailbed and put poison on them just to have my nails look cute for a month. You cannot afford to pay for someone to poison your mind about what is right or wrong. You certainly do not want to allow your mind to be poisoned into thinking that worldly things are your ultimate goals. After some time, you may or should realize what you heard was not right. Going back for another dose will only last for a limited time and cause more damage.

Tresa M. Sullivan

Time for Reflection: Encourage Yourself

Sipping Session Fifty-One

The Unintentional Gardener

Tresa M. Sullivan

Not everyone has a green thumb, yet many people set out to try their hand at raising something, whether it be flowers, plants, fruits, vegetables, or children. For some of us, 4H (Head, Heart, Hands, and Health) or science class gardening was our first attempt at growing something. While some of us were very focused and intentional, not everyone was successful. Some produced plants; others did not. My plants, whatever they were, grew despite my lack of interest in gardening. I did it for the grade. I followed the instructions, and my plants grew.

Although it had been well over 30 years since I last tried to raise something in a garden, a couple of years ago, I attempted to grow some tomatoes. Several people laughed at me and said I would not be successful, but I didn't care because I just wanted some tomatoes that did not taste like those in the store.

A man from my job shared his seedlings with me, and I bought everything else I needed to complete the task at hand, including a rolling tomato box. I planted the seedlings and took care to water them, give them sunlight, and protect them from pests. I used only potting soil so that I would not have to worry about weeds. It took a long time before the seedlings began to bloom. Other people were talking about how quickly their plants were growing, but mine seemed to lag behind. Eventually, they quit talking about theirs, and I heard nothing more unless I asked. Surprisingly, most of them said their plants did not do very well! By then, my little seedlings had taken off and were doing extremely well. I was picking bundles every day or two, and I did so for well over three months!

I showed my family and a couple of friends but did not brag at work. I still had no interest in gardening, but I wanted the tomatoes. At the end of the season, I pulled the dead plants and threw them away. I rolled my tomato box close to my back door and forgot all about them.

Although I had been successful, the following year, the squirrels helped me to make the decision not to try gardening again. So, my husband moved the box off the deck. I left to visit my mom for a couple of weeks, and when I returned home, I saw tomato plants had peeked their heads through a cloth on the box. I was tickled because I had no idea there would be anything left to grow. I did absolutely nothing more, but the plants were putting out about ten tomatoes every couple of days.

I prayed, "Lord, make me as my tomato plants. Let my actions and behaviors bloom beautifully because of who I am, not because I have to make an effort. Let my garden reap followers for You unintentionally because of what is within me, not the outward grooming. Let Your Word settle in my heart and soul so deeply that my actions today and from years ago will influence and draw people to You for years to come."

May your garden be forever fertile. I pray your tomato plants be perennials and never annuals.

Tresa M. Sullivan

Time for Reflection: Encourage Yourself

Sipping Session Fifty-Two

What You See is What You Get

I stopped wearing makeup about 30 years ago. I stopped cleaning my house just because I was expecting visitors about 20 years ago. I stopped saying things just to be kind about ten years ago. Okay. Honestly, I never said things just to be kind.

I always say, "I am a 'WYSIWYG' (pronounced "whizzy wig") woman." What that means is what you see is what you get. It takes too much effort to please others when doing so often displeases God. When you put your energy into pleasing God and find favor in His sight, He gives you favor in the sight of man. He will make your enemies fight for you. He will turn your foes into faithful followers.

As mean, introverted, and standoffish as some might say I am, I find people are drawn to me. I know it's not me, but the "Christ in me."

So, always be who you are and see what happens. Sometimes, people may not like it and treat you unfairly for it. When that happens, it may seem like punishment, but every single time it appeared that way to me, God made it a blessing. He made it the next step in my journey.

I can truly say I would not be where I am without every single falter (just being me and not exhibiting what others wished of me) that I have made.

Today's thought was a short story about me, Ms. WYSIWYG. That is a real IT acronym, one that I challenge you to put into action. Now, go and let everyone see exactly what they are getting!

TIPs for Sips

Time for Reflection: Encourage Yourself

Tresa M. Sullivan

Sipping Session Fifty-Three

Worry About Yourself

TIPs for Sips

Does it bother you when you are working hard and seem to be stuck in the same place, seeing absolutely no growth? You may have a project that seems to never get off the ground, or you know you deserve a promotion at work but do not get it. Does it seem like your neighbors or office mates are out of control? Are you struggling with your finances? Do you feel like you are not growing spiritually? Are you experiencing family drama with your spouse, children, or siblings? Sometimes, you may even feel like you are on the brink of a breakthrough, but instead, another problem arises.

When some (or all) of that is happening, you begin to ask, "Why?!" You look around and see other people prospering, and their good fortune seems to be spreading like wildfire. You become frustrated and wonder what you are doing wrong. You don't understand how the unjust appear to fare so well while you struggle...and struggle. Rest assured, it is not for us to worry about how the unjust is making out.

"Fret not thyself because of him who prospereth in his way, because of the man who bringeth wicked devices to pass." (Psalms 37:7)

We are reminded even further in Psalms 49:16-17:

"Don't be afraid when a man is made rich, when the glory of his house is increased. For when he dies, he shall carry nothing away. His glory shall not descend after him."

You were never told your personal journey would be easy, and you know God never gives you more than you can bear. Remember God's servant Job? He had done no wrong, yet the flesh fell from his bones, and he lost his family and so-called friends. Job's trials were to show the wicked one his faithfulness.

Everyone's journey belongs to that individual. Your trials and tribulations may be because you are asking for the wrong things. You may need to grow in your faith. Perhaps what you are asking could harm you or someone you love. You could quite possibly just need to listen to what God is telling you. You may be hardheaded. Whatever the case may be, you need to stop worrying about everyone else and worry about yourself. Ask God for direction and guidance. Then, listen and do as He says. Stop striking out on your own. Remember: God may allow the unjust to prosper for a time.

"For He maketh His sun to rise on the evil and on the good, and sendeth rain on the just and the unjust."
(Matthew 5:45)

So, as we are directed in James 5:7:

"Be patient, therefore, brethren, unto the coming of the Lord. Behold, the husbandman waiteth for the precious fruit of the earth, and hath long patience for it, until he receives the early and latter rain."

As the song goes, "God's got a blessing waiting on you."[e] My friend, if that blessing is nothing here on earth and is my ticket to Heaven, that is one for which I am willing to wait a lifetime! How about you?

TIPs for Sips

Time for Reflection: Encourage Yourself

Tresa M. Sullivan

Sipping Session Fifty-Four

Speaking of Rain...

TIPs for Sips

My friend, we just discussed the rain in James 5:7:

"Be patient, therefore, brethren, unto the coming of the Lord. Behold, the husbandman waiteth for the precious fruit of the earth, and hath long patience for it, until he receives the early and latter rain."

Rain is a powerful form of precipitation. It can relieve a drought, just as it can quickly cause flood damage. Rain can give life or take it away. I am sure you have probably heard the adage, "When it rains, it pours."[f] Sayings like that give rain a bad name. Here's the thing: The rain is not the problem; lack of preparation is.

When things seem to be going badly in your life, that is the time to come closer to God, not create distance between the two of you. Don't stop praying and thanking God for what you have. Whatever you need, still ask Him for it, but do not badger Him about it. He heard you the first time. Lean on your faith and continue to do your works. When He sends the rain, be ready. If it continues to pour, be like the ant: prepare in advance. Have your irrigation system ready to harness the good rain. Just as Noah prepared the ark, have your system ready so that when it floods, you either float, channel the rain to where it needs to go, or harness and save it until you need it.

There is nothing wrong with being "prayed up." The problem comes when you give up. If you give up in the storm, you may drown.

Tresa M. Sullivan

Time for Reflection: Encourage Yourself

Sipping Session Fifty-Five

How Deep Is Your Love?

Let me start by making it clear: "How deep is your love?" is a rhetorical question. I am not the one you need to answer.

Can you truly say you love your neighbor as you love yourself? Would you honestly turn the other cheek? Do you have faith the size of a mustard seed? Would you give/loan to an individual seven times over if they never repaid you? If you were sued and the complainant was awarded all you had except the clothes on your back, would you give them your clothes as well? Would you give your life for someone you never met or for someone who tortured and hated you?

Before you answer, don't get frustrated if your answer is no. Do not decide that you may as well give up because you do not think you will ever be able to answer yes to all of those questions. Why? Because God is a longsuffering, patient, loving, merciful, and forgiving God. If you were perfect, there would be no need for prayer or faith.

The potter knows every flaw and impurity you have. He patiently waits at the door for you to discover your shortcomings and ask for repair.

Now, don't get it twisted: If He shows you areas for improvement and you do not make a change, there will be trouble. Seek God's guidance while He may be found. The more you seek, the deeper love grows.

TIPs for Sips

Time for Reflection: Encourage Yourself

Tresa M. Sullivan

Sipping Session Fifty-Six

Five Senses

TIPs for Sips

We often take our senses for granted. We go through life casually half-listening to people and half-listening to God. We touch with our hands, but not our hearts. We taste food but say or do things in poor taste. We smell foods and fragrances as we go along but do not stop to smell the roses (or anything, for that matter). We look but do not see.

God blessed us with those five senses: touch, sight, hearing, smell, and taste. We should take time to thank God for them.

Let's explore the sense of sight. It has five sights within itself, in addition to vision. So, what does that really mean? We have:

1. Oversight: The action of overseeing, supervise. We have some authority over our daily lives but thank God; He has the oversight of all things.
2. Hindsight: Understanding of a situation or event, only after it has happened or developed. Let us thank God for the lessons learned.
3. Insight: The capacity to gain an accurate and deep, intuitive understanding of a person or thing. Be grateful for discernment.
4. Foresight: The ability to predict or the action of predicting what will happen or be needed in the future. Having an understanding and the ability to see when something is what you need or can do without.
5. Second Sight: The ability to see in the future or a sudden improvement in vision. What a blessing to suddenly see and understand what is going on—and have the wherewithal to take proper action!

With all of this depth into the sense of sight, how could we ever be ungrateful, narrowminded, or forgetful of God's blessings?

Tresa M. Sullivan

Today, let us start taking note of the senses God has given us and use them all wisely.

TIPs for Sips

Time for Reflection: Encourage Yourself

Tresa M. Sullivan

Sipping Session Fifty-Seven

The Clearing

In my mind, I found myself on a journey through a densely wooded place. When I could discern wrong from right was when the journey began.

At the time, I knew neither where the journey would end nor how much time I would spend. Not knowing what to pack, I took only a knapsack with just a few things within. I knew I would need water, food, clothes, and some comfortable shoes. Those were my personal effects, but what would I use for attacks? I would need a sword and shield to strike at my will, and perhaps I would need shelter.

Soon after my journey started, sin caught me off-guard, coming at me from every angle. I was lost and distraught, mangled and tangled, entrenched in the trees and vines…and the cares of this world. I then whipped out my sword — the Word of the Lord — and began to cut down the trees. It was all so much. I was overwhelmed, and the trees and leaves covered me.

Fearful and weary, I fell to my knees to ask for strength and forgiveness, which was only God's to dispense. I thought I was done and that Satan had won, then God took my knapsack. I was in utter disbelief and filled with grief. God opened the sack, then handed it back. He simply said, "Use these." I opened the sack, and it was now packed with strength, willpower, faith, courage, goodwill, hope, love, peace, mercy, and grace.

I sprang from my knees and chopped down the trees. I faltered from time to time, but I could see from afar just where I was going, and from whence I had come. As I looked back, I discovered my journey was a labor of love so endearing. Although I had struggled, I would not change a thing because I had finally reached the clearing.

Time for Reflection: Encourage Yourself

Sipping Session Fifty-Eight

If the Shoe Fits...

I guess I am back to idioms…

I am sure most of us have heard, "If the shoe fits, wear it." It is often used to tell someone, "If something is true of you, accept it and move on." You have also likely heard, "Until you walk in my shoes…" That means, "You do not know what you would do in my situation unless you have experienced it."

Let take both idioms a little further.

What if we stopped trying to wear other people's shoes and made our own comfortable? If you do something that is not quite right or not exactly as you should, fix your shoes. You may need to take a worn heel to the cobbler or slide in an insole or padding to stop the sliding.

Stay out of other people's shoes because shoes that are too big can cause as much damage as ones that are too small. Both can cause corns and chaffing — one from having too much give; the other from not enough.

So, if the shoe does fit, don't just wear it; wear it well. In other words, mind your own business when it is not prudent to interfere with other people's. Only provide guidance or advice or lend a hand when you are called upon or when it is within your purview.

TIPs for Sips

Time for Reflection: Encourage Yourself

Sipping Session Fifty-Nine

It's Not a Matter of Freedom, It's a Matter of Free Dum (Dum)

TIPs for Sips

"When I was a child, I spake as a child, I understood as a child, I thought as a child: but when I became a man, I put away childish things."
(1 Corinthians 13:11)

In the year 2020, I spent time trying to figure out a few things I believed should be common sense. In the midst of an epic pandemic and a nation torn apart by ignorance, I was bewildered at the behavior of many adults in the United States. I could understand a child not knowing how to behave, but a certain level of ignorance in adults was most perplexing.

When it comes to racism and wearing protective gear and equipment, I was baffled that some people did not know it was not a matter of freedom; it was a matter of free will. It bothered me that free dumdums did not understand. While freedom affords one liberation from restraint and power exerted by another without onerous obligations, free will is a voluntary choice not determined by prior causes.

Let's look at some childish things and behaviors most people outgrew (if they ever exhibited them at all):

1. As a child, wearing your shoes on the wrong foot: You knew it didn't feel quite right, but you did not let it bother you. It was a childish thing to do that caused no harm to anyone else or you. However, if someone told you that your shoes were on the wrong foot, you changed them.
2. Spitting on someone: It was nasty and did not cause you any harm, but it was a mean thing to do. If you did it, you knew it was wrong to do once you were told it was

improper. There was no physical harm to others, but it was hurtful emotionally.
3. Striking out and hitting people: It was both wrong and harmful to others. You were taught not to hit unless you were protecting yourself.

You are free to do all of those things. However, free will and common sense stop most people from doing them. The fact that you are free to do them because of your freedom, but free will prevents most people from doing them, is what confuses me about free dumdums who also do the following:

1. Incorrectly believe that race makes one person better than another.
2. Believe that jeopardizing the health, wellbeing, and lives of others during an epic pandemic is a "right."

If the previous two statements are inherently characteristic of you, your actions and behaviors are about as wise as:

1. Pouring water on a grease fire.
2. Letting a venomous snake roam free in the neighborhood because it is your pet.
3. Standing outside three feet away from an EF5 tornado because you think it is a hoax to steal your car.

What I am indicating here is that you need to elevate your understanding and stop thinking, speaking, and behaving like a child. It is not about what you have the freedom to do; it is about using free will to behave appropriately and not like a free dumdum.

TIPs for Sips

Time for Reflection: Encourage Yourself

Sipping Session Sixty

My Account

TIPs for Sips

I have gotten into the habit of checking my investment account daily. I check it when I wake, and I check again before retiring for the evening. My investment advisor is the greatest of all time because he handles so much more than my banking and financial needs. I refer to him as my Total Investment Advisor (TIA). He is helping me save for retirement. He never charges a fee, and He is never too busy with other clients to talk to me. In fact, my most valuable investment cannot be purchased with money. That is the one I really want to keep an eye on.

Sometimes, I get a little fretful and check throughout the day. I want to make sure I don't deplete the account. Every day, I try to make a measurable deposit of faith, love, good works, honesty, thanksgiving, hope, forgiveness, and even joy. However, I sometimes make a withdrawal that hurts me. I may say or do something that causes me not to be prepared if I were forced to retire unexpectedly. Since I want to retire comfortably, I try to make as many deposits and as few withdrawals as possible.

They used to say, "When E.F. Hutton talks, people listen."[8] Many people did take his financial advice, but his advice was not used for spiritual dividends.

God's Word is much more valuable than Hutton's. You better believe you are guaranteed a much better return on your investment, too!

Time for Reflection: Encourage Yourself

Sipping Session Sixty-One

Measured Steps, One Day at a Time

Tresa M. Sullivan

When I decided to dedicate my life to God, I wanted it to work like the flip of a switch. I wanted it to be like Genesis 1:3: "And God said, 'Let there be light: and there was light."

In my mind, I wanted my transformation to be instantaneous, like the story of Saul in the Book of Acts. I wanted to make a 180° change from my sinful ways immediately. I was not a terrible person. I had done only a few things wrong, but I was raised knowing that sin is sin, no matter the magnitude. I even cried and begged God to change me right away, calling out Saul as a prime example indicating that I knew God could do it. I even said to Him, "I know You can do it because there is nothing impossible nor too hard for You to do."

When I say pause and listen to what God has to say, I am not telling you to do so because it seems like a good thing to say; I am asking you to do so because I have learned to do just that. It was my, "You can't handle the truth!"[h] moment. God brought to my attention that I was not ready for what He did to and for Saul. Saul had been blinded for days after communicating with Jesus. In addition to the physical change, God changed Saul's heart and mind, but it was a process that did not take place immediately. What happened instantaneously was his acknowledgement of Jesus.

In my listening moment, I learned my journey is my journey, not Saul's or anyone else's. I learned mistakes are inevitable. I realized if I were strong enough and smart enough to do this all alone, there would be no need for various callings within the Word, nor would there be a need for the Holy Ghost. I learned that being saved is a lifestyle, not a magic trick. In that moment of listening, I learned this journey requires measured steps…one day at a time.

TIPs for Sips

Time for Reflection: Encourage Yourself

Tresa M. Sullivan

Sipping Session Sixty-Two

Before You Check Your Carry-On, Check Your Baggage

TIPs for Sips

Do you constantly find that everywhere you go, there is confusion? Is it always chaotic on the job or with your family and friends? Do you have to tell everybody how to think and get things done? Are you the one who holds it all together and, should something happen to you or you go away, everything is sure to fall apart? Do you feel like this life has you stressed to the max and that you need a break?

You are darned tooting you need a break! BUT before you check your carry-on at the airport, check your baggage to make sure you are not the carrier of the confusion and chaos you face. Clear your head because if you are the only one who sees things the way you do, you may be the problem.

If, indeed, you are the problem, unpack your baggage and everything you are carrying in your head because you are only running from yourself. The problem with running from yourself is that you always find yourself running into you.

Tresa M. Sullivan

Time for Reflection: Encourage Yourself

Sipping Session Sixty-Three

Which Will You Be?

Tresa M. Sullivan

We generally think of an ambassador as a diplomat authorized to represent a country in a foreign land. The ambassador is charged with promoting beneficial relationships and presenting the ideologies of his native land in a manner in which others are persuaded to believe and trust without coercion. It is clear that an ambassador carries information to share in hopes of convincing others in order to form allies.

As an ambassador, you must sometimes have complex and tough conversations, and you may, on occasion, have to admit you are wrong about something.

If you examine the word 'ambassador,' you will find there is another word that can be found embedded within. It is an animal that is sometimes called "a beast of burden": the ass. The ass carries a load, knowing not from whence it came or where it is going. It doesn't matter to the ass, as long as it is rewarded in the end.

You, too, are charged with carrying information. What will you do with it? Will you care and develop relationships that will lead others to the light and be an ambassador for God, or will you just be an ass?

This entry is not intended to offend anyone. The word 'ass' is used in the formal sense. Any other interpretation is purely coincidental.

TIPs for Sips

Time for Reflection: Encourage Yourself

Tresa M. Sullivan

Bonus

Remember When?

Do you remember the very first time you had a big secret you could not share with anyone? Do you remember how that felt? That is how your loved one feels now. He knows something he wishes he could share but cannot.

Do you remember the first secret you shared with your mom, dad, or best friend? You were so giddy. Your loved one is giddy now. He is sharing with our Heavenly Father every single thing that ever made him happy or sad—and that includes you.

Do you remember how it felt to see your mom or dad after your very first day of school? You may have been excited, anxious, and perhaps a bit apprehensive about leaving them at first, but by the end of the day, you were overjoyed to see them again. That is what your loved one is going through this very moment.

Do you remember your first or favorite toy, game, stuffed animal, or treasure—the one you wanted to have with you all the time? Remember what it felt like when it was tattered and worn, and you did not want to let it go? It ached so badly, but you knew it was time and you did what you had to do. Although nothing could ever replace it, you found something to fill the void. You and your loved one are in that same space now. Your loved one prepared himself and had let go of this life. You must be at peace with it, being comforted by the time you were afforded with him. He is assuming a new role in his new life now. I know you will find comfort and peace in fond, loving memories of the time he spent with you here. The love you shared remains and in time—with God's help—the memoires of what you shared will fill the hole in your heart.

Do you remember the first time you donned a brand-new outfit or new pair of shoes as a child, or perhaps a graduation cap and gown? You were so proud of yourself, it felt like your chest would burst wide open. Your loved one is experiencing that same euphoria as he dons his new and holy robe. He is admiring how perfectly it fits and how spotless it is, and he wishes everyone in the world could see it.

Do you remember how it felt to take a long trip to visit your loved ones? You were always so happy to see the family and was always so much fun! When the trip came to an end, you were sad to leave — but at the same time, it felt good to be home and to sleep in your own bed. That is how your loved one feels right now. He enjoyed his stay here immensely but knew it was time to go home where his rest is forever peaceful and ever-so-sweet.

Trust me: It is okay to cry when you have to say goodbye. *Just remember when…*

Know that all those good feelings you are drumming up when you remember when, your loved one is also experiencing them and would not have it any other way. So, pull out a memory book, photo album, or electronic picture frame, or call someone and bask in the glow of your family's love. Know that your loved one's spirit and love are with you always and his heart is about to burst with loving memories of you as he finds his place in Heaven — his new **HOME**.

Your strength comes from the Lord.

Your courage comes from within.

Your comfort comes from thoughts and prayers of family and friends.

Your peace comes from cherished memories.

May God bless and forever keep you in His perfect will.

About the Author

Tresa M. Sullivan was born in Hayti, Missouri — a small town in the state's southeastern region. It was there where her parents taught her that being right and living right are two different things and that the latter is more important. They also taught her nothing is more important than her soul.

Winter is Tresa's favorite season. Her hobbies include writing, learning to sketch, and photography. She is a lifelong learner who never stops seeking to learn something new.

Tresa now lives on the East Coast with her husband of 32 years. They have two sons and a pup named Benji.

Appendix

a. Walter White quote: Testimony of Walter White, North 6th Street Church of God in Christ, Hayti, Missouri.
b. "Jesus Is on the Mainline" by Ryland Peter Cooder.
c. "The House by the Side of the Road" by Sam Walter Foss.
d. "Something About the Name Jesus" by The Rance Allen Group.
e. "God's Got a Blessing" by Lee Williams and the Spiritual QCs.
f. "When it Rains, it Pours": Morton Salt Slogan.
g. "When E.F. Hutton speaks, people listen": E.F. Hutton commercial.
h. "You can't handle the truth" quote. "A Few Good Men," 1992; produced by Aaron Sorkin.

www.ingramcontent.com/pod-product-compliance
Lightning Source LLC
LaVergne TN
LVHW011934070526
838202LV00054B/4639